Chris McGarvey is an experienced food lawyer who has been involved in animal feed law for many years. Dual qualified in both England and Wales, and Alberta, Canada, he has a professional interest in food and feed law and is a Director in the Regulatory and Compliance Team at Walker Morris LLP.

Chris spent some eight years at the Food Standards Agency and led the in-house Legal Team through Brexit, the Pandemic, and supply-chain challenges associated with the conflict in Ukraine. He lives in Cambridgeshire.

A Practical Guide to the Law of Animal Feed in the United Kingdom

A Practical Guide to the Law of Animal Feed in the United Kingdom

Christopher M McGarvey
LLB; PG Dip; LLM
Solicitor of the Senior Courts (England and Wales)
Barrister and Solicitor (Alberta, Canada)

Law Brief Publishing

Published 2025 by Law Brief Publishing, an imprint of Law Brief Publishing Ltd
30 The Parks
Minehead
Somerset
TA24 8BT

www.lawbriefpublishing.com

Paperback: 978-1-916698-92-5

This book is dedicated to my partner, Tina, my children Abigail and James, my grandchildren, Jaxon and Carson, and my stepchildren, Matan and Tami – with love always.

PREFACE

I have been involved in the practice of animal feed law for many years, now. I would readily confess to not having had much affection for it at first. But the topic grew on me. And the knowledge, wisdom and kindness of colleagues who, over the years, shared their insights about feed law with me made a lasting and wholly beneficial impression upon me.

I had wished – in first encountering the topic of feed law as a junior lawyer at the Food Standards Agency – to have had recourse to a simple, or first principles, legal text of the kind I hope is represented by this book. It would have made life easier to see feed law (or much of it) gathered together in one place and accompanied by some explanation of what it was broadly all about. I hope that, for those feeling a similar need for simplicity, this book goes some way towards meeting it.

Feed law is, of course, an important topic not only from the point of view of human health, but also because we love our animals in the United Kingdom. We want to know that, whether they are farm animals or domestic pets, they are well cared-for, and that their many and varied nutritional needs are met. Feed law is designed to help to achieve just that. It represents an important element of the agri-food legal framework in both the United Kingdom and Europe and, for those lawyers or officials involved in advising upon or operating the framework, is a topic which (in my view) rewards study and examination.

I would like to thank all those colleagues who I have worked with, in both the public sector and in private practice, for their help and encouragement over the years. I have worked with some amazing scientists, policy specialists, lawyers, and enforcement officials – all of whom worked hard to achieve the positive societal outcomes mentioned above. You know who you are.

I would also like to thank Tim Kevan and Garry Wright of Law Brief Publishing for seeing potential in the idea of this book, and for their support in making it a reality.

In closing this preface, I have to mention some important points, which are these.

This book focuses on legislation and case law which applies throughout the United Kingdom. However, readers should be aware that, as a devolved matter, animal feed law may vary as between England, Wales, Scotland and Northern Ireland. While differences are generally minor, they do exist, and readers should always identify the precise law which applies to the jurisdiction with which they are concerned, using the general descriptions in this book as a starting point.

I also must point out that the views expressed in this book are wholly mine, as are any errors and omissions.

And finally, I can say that I have tried to state the law as at 1 May 2025.

Christopher M McGarvey
June 2025

CONTENTS

CHAPTER ONE

DEVELOPMENT OF FEED LAW

Introduction

In this introductory chapter, we briefly examine the development of United Kingdom (UK) law relating to animal feed and how it has gradually evolved to form the somewhat complex set of provisions we see today.

The end of the nineteenth century and the beginning of the twentieth century witnessed two changes which created the framework which largely endures to the present day. The first of these was industrialisation of feed production, and the increased volume of production and sophistication that that brought with it. The second was a relative inversion in the importance of contract law and statute law as the means by which the quality and other attributes of feed were determined. While this inversion did not quite turn *caveat emptor* (let the buyer beware) into *caveat venditor* (let the seller beware), the greater role which regulation played in the commercial supply of animal feed was of considerable significance in setting standards and clarifying expectations about feed safety.

As with many other areas of public policy where increasingly sophisticated economic and commercial practices created perceived imbalances and sometimes, criminality, Parliament has seen fit to intervene in the regulation of animal feed on numerous occasions. Intervention has often been prompted by major developments of various kinds, including natural events such as unforeseen outbreaks of animal disease, as well as political events, such as the UK's joining, and eventual leaving, of the European Union (**EU**).

The UK has also responded, over the years, to developments at an international level, either through promoting global standards for animal feed as part of its membership of the EU trading bloc, or by meeting its own international trading partners' requirements for the quality of animal feed. Trading objectives have impacted, and continue to impact, on the development of domestic feed law. A brief examination of these international factors is therefore helpful, at this early stage, to set the context for much of what follows in later chapters.

What can undoubtedly be said at the outset about animal feed law in the UK is that, unlike certain more visible areas of regulation, such as in the health service, education, or local government – where piecemeal legal developments are from time-to-time incorporated into consolidated Acts of Parliament – the law relating to animal feed has tended to develop in discrete strands or layers without any serious attempt at consolidation.

Regrettably, this means that animal feed law remains spread across various parts of the statute book often making the nailing down of the answer to a specific query, quite the challenge.

This book provides something of a guide map, so that the reader can begin to begin to trace out those legal provisions which can answer the particular point about animal feed with which they may be grappling.

It is important to stress at the outset that this book focuses on legislation and case law which applies throughout the UK. However, readers should be aware that, as a devolved matter, animal feed law may vary as between England, Wales, Scotland and Northern Ireland. While differences are generally minor, they do exist, and readers should always identify the precise law which applies to the jurisdiction with which they are concerned, perhaps using the general descriptions in this book as a starting point.

Early legislation

Regulatory provision relating to animal feed gradually began to take shape from the end of the nineteenth century onwards. The first piece of legislation, aimed at preventing adulteration of animal feed, was the Fertilisers and Feeding Stuffs Act 1893. This Act made it an offence, among other things, to sell feed for cattle containing any ingredient 'deleterious' to cattle, or to which had been added any ingredient 'worthless' for feeding purposes and not disclosed at the time of sale. These provisions were updated over time but have now disappeared from the statute book.

European Union law

Development of feed law has also taken place at a European level. For the period 1973 to 2020 – during which time the UK was a member of the EU and its predecessor organisations – numerous measures were adopted relating to the composition and marketing of animal feed. These included various Directives which the UK faithfully implemented by way of domestic secondary legislation made under the European Communities Act 1972 (**ECA**).

During the later period of the UK's membership, the EU passed directly applicable regulations in respect of feed, including its marketing, composition, use and, notably, hygiene, with this final topic being an aspect of safety management to which domestic feed law had, until then, paid little attention.

These EU regulations did not need any implementing regulations under the ECA before they could be relied upon in domestic law. But as EU regulations do not generally specify enforcement measures – instead relying on member States to provide for enforcement using measures available in their own national legal systems – it was necessary for the four nations of the UK to pass domestic legislation to deal with enforcement.

While during its membership of the EU, the UK no doubt made compromises in relation to the detail of the feed legislation which was eventually adopted by the EU, it would be fair to say that, at a philosophical level, both the EU and the UK shared the view that feed was, and is, an important part of the human food chain and deserving of regulatory intervention.

EU Exit

After forty-seven years' membership, the UK left the EU on 31 January 2020. EU law continued to apply in the UK during a transition period which ended at 11pm GMT on 31 December 2020. In anticipation of leaving, the UK passed the European Union (Withdrawal) Act 2018 (**EUWA**) which, broadly speaking, 'saved' much of the EU law, which would otherwise have been repealed, and turned it into domestic law. This domestic law (now known as "*assimilated law*") could then, under less pressure of time, be added to, changed, or repealed/revoked as the UK (or its devolved nations) thought fit. Had this step not been taken, the regulatory framework for animal feed – along with many other areas of economic activity – would have been left in an incomplete and incoherent state and its important objectives, compromised.

As with other areas of assimilated law, extensive changes were made to EU feed law by statutory instruments made under the EUWA so that it worked properly after EU Exit. These changes did not alter the policy underpinning the law, but did make certain necessary amendments including, for instance, to the identity of bodies fixed with functions under the law, so that, in future, these bodies were UK bodies rather than EU bodies to which the UK no longer had access.

One of the seemly intractable problems of EU Exit was the status of Ireland. Ireland was the location of the UK's only land border with the EU. While in many other parts of Europe, a hard border with control posts and inspection of goods and people passing through them would be uncontroversial, Ireland was different. A hard border between the Republic of Ireland and the British province of Northern Ireland was, politically, highly sensitive. It was also argued to be prohibited by the terms of the Belfast (or Good Friday) Agreement, which had been made in 1998 between the Irish and UK governments and the various political parties active in the province.

The Northern Ireland Protocol/Windsor Framework

Given the difficulties which a hard border on the island of Ireland would have created, special provision was made for Northern Ireland – the Northern Ireland Protocol (**Protocol**) – by which EU law would continue to apply there. The continued application of the Protocol is subject to periodic confirmation by a democratic vote of residents of Northern Ireland. The Protocol proved problematic in practice, as well as politically sensitive, and amendments were made to it by the Windsor Framework in 2023.

Among other things, the Windsor Framework allows a number of retail products (including certain pre-packaged pet food items) to be moved from Great Britain to Northern Ireland even though they may not comply with EU Law. However, with the exception of certain pre-packaged pet food, animal feed moved from Great Britain to Northern

Ireland is not covered by the Windsor Framework easements and is subject to the full application of EU Law and checks at the GB/Northern Ireland border before it can be placed on the market in Northern Ireland.

International considerations

Following EU Exit, the UK and EU, as major trading partners, negotiated and implemented a free trade agreement known as the Trade and Cooperation Agreement (**TCA**). Under the TCA, the parties agreed tariff free mutual trade of many goods (including animal feed) and some mutual market access for services.

The TCA also deals with what are known as sanitary and phytosanitary standards (**SPS**). In broad terms, these are the rules and standards which countries put in place to identify and mitigate the biological, and other, hazards which plants and animals create, and which aim to provide protections against the inadvertent introduction of contagious diseases and other pathogens to which uncontrolled import and export of plants and animals might otherwise give rise. Animal feed – whether of plant or animal origin (or both) – falls squarely within the category of goods to which SPS standards are directed.

Sanitary and phytosanitary standards

SPS considerations are an important aspect of any free trade arrangement and serve to condition and qualify a country's commitment to allow free movement of goods into its territory. In broad terms, World Trade Organisation (**WTO**) rules require a member's SPS standards to be based firmly on science and to be no more restrictive of free trade than is necessary. So far as the TCA between the EU and the UK is concerned, each party maintains its own SPS standards and, at the time of writing, does not recognise the other party's SPS standards as offering equivalence in terms of the quality of protection they provide.

The practical effect of a lack of recognised equivalence is that there is no free movement of animal feed between the EU and UK; rather each party applies some specific and demanding conditions at the border. These conditions include the supply of Export Health Certificates (**EHCs**) in respect of feed containing products of animal origin (which need to be completed by a veterinary surgeon); pre-notification of the arrival of affected feed at the border, inspection of documentation relating to the feed, and physical inspection of the feed itself by appropriately qualified border officials. These documents and checks add considerable cost and delay to the process of import and export, and generally make for higher prices for the goods in question. A brief consideration of how the law applies to the import and export of animal feed can be found in Chapter Four.

The EU "reset"

In May 2025, the UK and EU announced that they hope to negotiate a new SPS agreement which would reduce or eliminate many of these documents and checks. As part of the discussions, known in the UK as the EU "reset", the UK has indicated that it may be willing to accept, as part of its domestic law, relevant elements of EU law relating to plants, animals and their derivatives (which would include animal feed). The UK has also indicated that it might also be willing (subject to limited exceptions) to agree that these EU laws will be subject to periodic amendment by the EU – a process known as "*dynamic alignment*". It does not appear that the EU is willing to agree to the UK having any role in the development and enactment of relevant EU law, and the UK appears to accept that, under the arrangements, the final arbiter of the meaning and effect of the EU law in question will be the Court of Justice of the European Union.

Critically, if a new SPS is reached in these terms, it will, once again, make EU law of direct relevance to feed law practitioners in the UK, and could change the legal landscape for animal feed in a way which seemed unlikely following EU Exit.

Conclusion

The law relating to animal feed is complex and has developed over many years. The main elements of feed law are now made up of assimilated law. This is law which was previously EU law (or domestic law made to implement or enforce EU law) and which has now been made part of our domestic law. However, some purely domestic legal provisions remain, most notably provisions made by, or under, the Agriculture Act 1970 (**AA 1970**).

Regrettably, there has been no real attempt at a consolidation of the various feed law provisions which apply in the UK and finding the answer to a particular food law query can be a challenge. This challenge has been made all the more difficult by EU Exit, and the volume of secondary legislation which it generated. Nevertheless, the EU Exit legislation forms an important part of the feed law framework in the UK, and ensures that EU law continues to work in a new, exclusively domestic, setting.

We hope that this book makes the process of finding the relevant feed law provisions simpler, by explaining where the main elements of feed law can be found and the reasons why the legislation takes the particular – and sometimes unexpected – form that it takes.

CHAPTER TWO

FEED LAW BASICS

Introduction

In this chapter, we attempt to set out some basic legal concepts adopted by feed law, and to describe some of its main policy objectives.

We also introduce readers to the main sources of feed law, being the Agriculture Act 1970 (**AA 1970**), the Food Safety Act 1990, the Food Standards Act 1999, and General Food Law in the form of Assimilated Regulation (EC) No. 178/2002.

These main enactments contain the key legal definitions which create the scope and reach of feed law, and which set out the boundary lines which separate it from its somewhat 'grander' relative in the form of food law.

Policy objectives

This book is not intended as a detailed examination of the policies underpinning feed law. These are many and varied and take in a wide range of matters associated with agricultural, environmental, economic and trade concerns.

However, what we can certainly say is that the current legal framework for feed recognises that feed given to food producing animals has an effect on human health. The effect can, of course, be good or bad. A bad effect usually comes about due to the manifestation of certain risks, which can be physical, biological or chemical in nature. But so far as human health is concerned, it is the latter two of these risks which are of most significance. We briefly examine these, below.

Biological risks

One of the most devastating agricultural events in recent times – the development of Bovine Spongiform Encephalitis (**BSE**) in the UK herd – was almost certainly brought about by the since banned practice of including ruminant animal proteins (usually meat and bone-meal) in feed fed to cattle. BSE was, of course, implicated in the development of Creutzfeldt-Jakob disease (**vCJD**) in people who had consumed affected beef.

Both diseases create what is known as a "*prion*". Prions are misshaped or misfolded proteins which build up in the brain of the disease carrier and cause healthy brain cells to die. Symptoms may take time to develop, but the effects of the disease can then progress rapidly leading to significant debilitation and death.

A case in which the seriousness with which the authorities view the ban on inclusion of animal proteins in feed was examined, is the Irish Supreme Court case of *Albatros Feeds v Minister for Agriculture and Food* [2007] Eu. L.R. 485. Here, the relevant government minister had purported to direct the claimant to recall a consignment of corn gluten intended for use as animal feed and to seize and detain the feed. The minister's action had been a response to sampling and analysis of the feed which had shown that it contained bone fragments, creating a risk that the feed could spread BSE. While, in the event, the Supreme Court of Ireland held that the minister had no power to act as she had purported to act, and dismissed her appeal, the case showed the resolve of the authorities to act firmly in cases where breach of the ban is detected.

To similar effect is the case of *Bellio Fratelli Srl v Prefettura di Treviso* (C-286/02). Here, a Feed Business Operator (**FeBO**) was convicted of importing contaminated fish flour into Italy from Norway. The flour was intended for use in pig food but was found to be contaminated with 0.1 per cent animal bone fragments. The Court of Justice of the European Union held that the relevant Commission Decisions dealing with the mitigation of risks relating to Transmissible Spongiform Encephalopathies (**TSEs**) did not allow the presence of the contaminant, at any level, and that the destruction of the flour was a preventive measure provided for by the relevant Decision.

Chemical risks

The risks to human health associated with animal feed go beyond biological risks. For example, dairy cattle who consume grass in a field where car batteries have been discarded may have ingested heavy metals such as lead and cadmium, which could taint the milk obtained from the animal and harm human consumers in the process.

Even careful animal husbandry can still create hazards. For instance, some veterinary medicines aimed at protecting the health and welfare of farmed animals can remain in an animal's body for some time after administration, and create a risk to human health if food derived from that animal is consumed while traces of the medicine are still present.

It is with these factors in mind that policy makers in both the UK and the EU approach feed as being part of the human food chain and seek to ensure that the law regulates the composition and purity of feed as a matter of public as well as animal health.

Non-food producing animals

While domestic legislation has for some years concerned itself with feed for non-food producing animals (see the discussion of the AA 1970, below), it was not until more recent times (since 2010), that animal feed legislation in the EU was extended to include pet food, even though the risk to human health associated with pet food is, in relative terms, marginal. Nevertheless, the recitals to Regulation (EC) No. 767/2009 on the placing on the market and use of feed state that:

"Given the risk of contamination of the feed and food chain, it is appropriate that this Regulation apply to feed for both food and non-food producing animals, including wild animals.".

A useful illustration of how feed law now impacts on the sale of pet food is to be found in the case of *R (on the application of Fold Hill Foods Ltd) v Food Standards Agency* [2023] EWHC 2271, a fuller discussion of which appears in Chapter Three.

The main sources of feed law

In terms of the legal framework itself, the law governing animal feed is contained across a range of assimilated and domestic legal measures, including regulations made under powers contained in Part IV of the AA 1970.

The Agriculture Act 1970

Although now of some vintage, the AA 1970 remains of considerable importance as a source of feed law. In fact, with the changes recently brought about by the Retained EU Law (Revocation and Reform) Act 2023, which, among other things, effectively reverse the doctrine of

EU law supremacy, by making assimilated law subordinate to domestic statute law in the event of any incompatibility between the two, the AA 1970 may now enjoy something of a renewed lease of life.

The AA 1970, in its original form, covered a wide range of policy matters, including the creation of an Eggs Authority, farm grants, smallholdings, and flood warning systems. Much of the AA 1970 has now been repealed. But it is Part IV of the AA 1970 which is of interest to us, and that Part remains in full force and effect.

Part IV deals with fertilisers and feeding stuffs. Feeding stuff is defined as:

> *a) a product of vegetable or animal origin in its natural state (whether fresh or preserved);*
>
> *b) a product derived from the industrial processing of such a product; or*
>
> *c) an organic or inorganic substance, used singly or in a mixture (and whether or not containing additives);*
>
> *for oral feeding to pet animals and such descriptions of animals as may be prescribed being animals which, or kinds of which, are commonly kept for the production of food, wool, skins or fur or for the purpose of their use in the farming of land.*

Part IV also deals, variously, with the appointment of enforcement authorities, inspectors and agricultural analysts; sampling and analysis, prosecutions, and confers power on ministers to make regulations governing the composition, content or function of feeding stuffs.

The regulation-making power, at section 74A, has been used extensively over the years to make detailed regulatory provision relating to animal feed, albeit its scope has not always been wide enough to provide for implementation or enforcement of certain EU feed laws. In this latter case, ministers have typically drawn on the wide regulation-making powers which were contained in the (now repealed) European Communities Act 1972 (**ECA**) section 2(2).

So far as substantive regulation of feed is concerned, section 68 sets out that a seller of feed must give the buyer a statutory statement which describes the nature, substance and quality of the feed, as well as instructions relating to its storage, handling and use. Subject to a minor exception, the failure to provide the statutory statement, as required by the section, is an offence.

Section 70 deals with the use of particular terms in statutory statements and information given to buyers of feed. If a seller uses terms to describe feed to which terms a particular meaning has been given in legislation, then a failure of the feed to comply with that particular meaning is an offence. The section also provides a buyer with a common law right in the form of a contractual warranty, being a warranty which the seller will breach should they fail to supply feed which complies with the particular meaning. It is important to be aware that, to the extent to which Regulation (EC) No. 767/2009 applies to the seller, then the offence elements of section 70 are disapplied. The presence of the contractual warranty implied by the section is unaffected.

Section 71 is similar in effect but deals with the attributes of the feed which the seller claims for it, and censures the seller for the use of the claim unless the attribute is described in accordance with delegated legislation governing the attribute. This section now appears to have fallen into disuse.

Section 72 is an important section. It provides for a statutory warranty of fitness of the feeding stuff to be implied in a contract of sale. We examine the warranty in more detail in Chapter Four.

The Food Safety Act 1990 and the Food Standards Act 1999

Powers for ministers to make provisions regulating animal feed are also to be found in the Food Safety Act 1990, section 16. This section empowers ministers to make provision for requiring, prohibiting or regulating the presence in 'food sources' of any specified substances. Under the 1990 Act, a "*food source*" is "*any growing crop or live animal, bird or fish from which food is intended to be derived (whether by harvesting, slaughtering, milking, collecting eggs or otherwise)*".

And, in a similar way, ministers are empowered under the Food Standards Act 1999, section 30, to make orders regulating any animal feedingstuff or anything done to or in relation to, or with a view to the production of, any animal feedingstuff.

It is interesting to note that the regulation-making powers in these two important Acts of Parliament have rarely been used in connection with animal feed regulation. Whether that will change in the new, post-EU Exit, era remains to be seen.

General Food Law Regulation (EC) No. 178/2002

The principal definition of feed is contained in Assimilated Regulation (EC) No. 178/2002 (commonly known as "*General Food Law*") where, at Article 3(4), it states:

> *'feed' (or 'feedingstuff') means any substance or product, including additives, whether processed, partially processed, or unprocessed, intended to be used for oral feeding to animals.*

And so far as those persons whose actions in feeding animals are intended to be regulated by the feed law framework, Article 3(5) provides that a:

> *"'feed business' means any undertaking whether for profit or not and whether public or private, carrying out any operation of production, manufacture, processing, storage, transport or distribution of feed including any producer producing, processing or storing feed for feeding to animals on his own holding.".*

At Article 3(6):

> *"'feed business operator' means the natural or legal persons responsible for ensuring that the requirements of food law are met within the feed business under their control.".*

The definition of "*food law*" runs through much of the legal framework for feed, and its definition, found at Article 3(1) is particularly broad:

> *"'food law' means the laws, regulations and administrative provisions governing food in general, and food safety in particular ... it covers any stage of production, processing and distribution of food, and also of feed produced for, or fed to, food-producing animals...".*

These definitions create the foundations upon which feed law is built. Feed covers all manner of raw and processed substances, including additives which includes things such as preservatives, colours and antibiotics, fed by mouth to animals. And feed businesses cover a wide spectrum of organisations – both public and private sector entities – and captures the whole supply chain from manufacture through to distribution.

These definitions, taken from General Food Law Regulation, have held sway over feed law for many years. However, to the extent to which there is any inconsistency between them and any definitions in applicable domestically derived law, those inconsistencies must now be resolved in favour of domestic law. This is a consequence of important provisions made by the Retained EU Law (Revocation and Reform) Act 2023. These provisions represent, in effect, a reversal of the doctrine of supremacy of EU law which has for so long been a feature of domestic legal system.

Conclusion

In this chapter, we have noted that one of the important policy objectives pursued by feed law concerns the effects which animal feed can have on human health.

We have also described where the main sources of feed law can be found and some of the key definitions which they contain.

With these building blocks in place, we can now go on to explore some of the main elements of feed law, including matters relating to safety, composition and labelling.

CHAPTER THREE

GENERAL FEED LAW OBLIGATIONS

Introduction

The bedrock of current feed law is to be found in the General Food Law Regulation (EC) No. 178/2002.

The Regulation sets out some clear obligations for feed businesses and establishes some baselines relating to safety, composition and labelling which must be met before feed can lawfully be placed on the market. It is an important enactment and feed practitioners should familiarise themselves with it.

General Food Law Regulation (EC) No. 178/2002

Perhaps the first point to note in relation to feed is that, as with food, the Regulation, at Article 17, unambiguously places primary legal responsibility for feed law compliance upon Feed Business Operators (**FeBOs**) at all stages of production, processing and distribution. So far as relevant, the Article is in the following terms:

> *"... [F]eed business operators at all stages of production, processing and distribution within the businesses under their control shall ensure that ... feeds satisfy the requirements of food law which are relevant to their activities and shall verify that such requirements are met."*

In practice, this means that it is not possible for a FeBO who, for instance, simply distributes feed, to attempt to shift legal responsibility for the safety of feed to its product suppliers, whether as a matter of contract or otherwise. The responsibility to ensure that the feed meets the requirements of food law, and obligation to verify that the responsibility is met, rests with a FeBO at the point at which it places its feed on the market.

The feed safety requirement

Then, arguably what is the main obligation imposed upon FeBOs is set out in Article 15 of the General Food Law. It is as follows:

1. *Feed shall not be placed on the market or fed to any food-producing animal if it is unsafe.*

2. *Feed shall be deemed to be unsafe for its intended use if it is considered to:*

    - *have an adverse effect on human or animal health;*

    - *make the food derived from food-producing animals unsafe for human consumption.*

While many practitioners will see the similarities with the definition of unsafe food, to be found at Article 14 of General Food Law, the inclusion of the words *"...for its intended use..."* marks a distinction in Article 15 from its food counterpart. The inclusion of these words appears to reflect the fact that feed intended for one species of animal could, of course, be perfectly safe for consumption by that species but very harmful if fed to another species. That, of course, is not a difficulty for food law.

As in the case of food, Article 15 goes on to make clear that if feed which is unsafe is part of a batch, lot or consignment, there is a legal presumption that the whole batch, lot or consignment is similarly unsafe. This presumption can be displaced (in legal terms "rebutted") if, following suitable analysis, there is no evidence that the whole batch, lot or consignment is unsafe.

Article 15 also provides that, so far as feed complies with any specific legislative requirements which apply to it, it shall be deemed to be safe. This provision is interesting because it does not go on to provide for the converse proposition – that feed is deemed to be unsafe if it fails to comply with any such specific requirements.

This raises a strong implication that a failure to comply with any specific feed law requirements does not mean, in and of itself, that the affected feed is unsafe; in these circumstances an enforcement authority may still have to prove with suitable scientific evidence that the feed is actually unsafe before an offence relating to the safety of the feed under Article 15 could be successfully prosecuted.

Placing on the market

It is important to note that legal obligations in relation to unsafe feed can occur long before the point of sale. Indeed, the legal obligation can arise even if feed is given away for free. This is because the obligation occurs at the point at which feed is "*placed on the market*". By virtue of Article 3(8) of the General Food Law, placing on the market means the holding of feed for the purposes of sale, and the transfer of ownership of the feed, whether free or charge or not.

An important supporting obligation is contained in Article 20 of the General Food Law. This Article requires a FeBO to immediately takes steps with withdraw a feed from the market where the FeBO has suspicion that the feed is unsafe and, at the same time, to inform its local feed authority of the withdrawal. The FeBO must also inform its customers of the withdrawal and the reasons for it, and if necessary, invite customers to return the feed to ensure that animal and human health is protected.

A recent case which examined the extent of the FeBO's obligations in relation to the safety of pet food and the requirement to recall unsafe pet food is *R. (on the application of Fold Hill Foods Ltd) v Food Standards Agency* [2023] EWHC 2271. Here, following an outbreak of feline pancytopaenia (a serious and often deadly disease in cats), Fold Hill Food recalled a number of its brands accompanied by a Product Recall Information Notice issued by the Food Standards Agency (**FSA**). Fold Hill's complaint in the case was that there was no proven link between the outbreak and its products and that the FSA had threatened to compel it to perform a recall if Fold Hill did not do it voluntarily. Fold Hill also complained that the information which the FSA had issued to the public about the recalls was irrational and unlawful. The Administrative Court dismissed Fold Hill's challenge on both grounds, finding that, on the evidence, there had been no threat of the kind alleged by Fold Hill and that, as a matter of law, the FSA had not acted irrationally or unlawfully in relation to its public updates.

In terms of labelling, a baseline requirement for the presentation of feed for sale is set by Article 16. This sets an overarching requirement that labelling, packaging, display arrangements and supporting information – however conveyed – must not mislead consumers.

Traceability

Finally, we cannot leave the General Food Law Regulation without considering the provision it makes in relation to the traceability of feed. The ability of a FeBO to act quickly in the event of a recall or withdrawal of feed, and the corresponding need of enforcement authorities to be able to map-out supply chains in helping to manage feed safety incidents, would be seriously impeded if FeBOs did not keep records of businesses from whom and to whom feed has been supplied.

The Regulation sets out the traceability requirements at Article 18 as follows:

> "*1. The traceability of ... feed ... and any other substance intended to be, or expected to be, incorporated into a ... feed shall be established at all stages of production, processing and distribution.*
>
> *2. ... [F]eed business operators shall be able to identify any person from whom they have been supplied with ... a feed ... or any substance intended to be, or expected to be, incorporated into a ... feed.*
>
> *To this end, such operators shall have in place systems and procedures which allow for this information to be made available to the competent authorities on demand.*
>
> *3. ... [F]eed business operators shall have in place systems and procedures to identify the other businesses to which their products have been supplied. This information shall be made available to the competent authorities on demand.*".

These requirements are generally known as the "*one-step forward, one-step back*" principle. In simple terms, the principle makes clear that a

FeBO is not expected to be able to describe its complete supply-chain, but must, at a minimum, be able to state from whom it has acquired a feed or feed ingredient, and to whom (if the recipient is a business) it has supplied a feed or feed ingredient.

Conclusion

The basic legal requirements which apply to feed are simply stated and relatively neatly expressed in the General Food Law Regulation (EC) No. 178/2002. They concern safety, composition and labelling. They constitute the minimum standards which feed businesses must meet which placing feed on the market.

The Regulation also imposes some important obligations on feed businesses so far as feed is found not to comply with these minimum standards. In particular, where a feed is unsafe, feed businesses must actively withdraw and recall feed from the market and inform the relevant authorities of the circumstances.

CHAPTER FOUR

OTHER LEGISLATION AFFECTING FEED

Introduction

In this chapter, we will look at the various other enactments which affect feed. Taken as a whole, these measures can appear bewildering. But they follow a well-trodden path and can be deciphered with some time and effort. Indeed, once a basic understanding of the structure of these measures is to hand, a relatively harmonious picture emerges. That is, perhaps, all the more surprising given the complicated interactions between domestic and EU measures by which the existing legal framework came into being.

While a later chapter of this book is given over to the subject of official controls and enforcement of feed law, so far as the import of feed into GB is concerned we will look briefly at enforcement in this chapter. This is because the interaction of feed law with legislation affecting imports is complex and best examined as a whole, rather than decoupled for separate discussion.

Composition, marketing and use of feed

Assimilated Regulation (EC) No. 767/2009

The first of these other enactments to be examined is Assimilated Regulation (EC) No. 767/2009 on the placing on the market and use of feed. This Regulation imposes a range of specific obligations on Feed Business Operators (**FeBOs**) relating to the composition, marketing and use of feed, including provision relating to safety, the content of feed additives, the prohibition of certain materials for use in feed (including animal waste, household waste, wood, sawdust, hides which have been treated with tanning materials, and packaging from the agri-food industry).

Regulation 767/2009 also sets out important general mandatory labelling and information requirements relating to feed. These include placing on the label information as to:

- Whether the feed is a feed material, a complete feed or a complementary feed.
- The name or business name and the address of the FeBO responsible for the labelling.
- The approval number of the premises producing the feed (if available).
- The batch and lot numbers.
- The net quantity.
- Any feed additives.
- The moisture content.

Depending upon the nature of the feed, the Regulation goes on to set out additional specific labelling requirements for feed materials, compound feeds, feed for particular nutritional purposes, pet food, and some non-compliant feeds (these feeds may contain contaminants capable of removal after processing and the labelling should make that clear).

The Regulation also deals with the packaging of feed and, with a considerable number of exceptions, sets a general rule that feed must be packaged in sealed containers before it is placed on the market.

Catalogue of Feed Materials

In addition, Regulation 767/2009 creates a statutory Catalogue of Feed Materials (**Catalogue**) for the UK, the use of which is voluntary, but the name of a feed material listed in the Catalogue may be used only on condition that all relevant provisions of the Catalogue are complied with. The Catalogue is currently maintained and published by the UK Feed Chain Task Force, which is made up of a number of UK animal feed trade associations.

Feed hygiene

Assimilated Regulation (EC) No. 183/2005

While composition and labelling of feed has a long domestic history of regulation, the same cannot be said of feed hygiene. This changed in 2005, when the EU adopted Regulation (EC) No. 183/2005 laying down requirements for feed hygiene.

Assimilated Regulation (EC) No. 183/2005, as it now is, sets down standards relating to the transport and storage of feed, maintenance of equipment, the training of personnel, and the keeping of records.

The Regulation distinguishes between activities which take place at the point of primary production (which includes the growing, harvesting, milking, and rearing of animals) and activities which take place later in the agri-food chain, i.e. during the processing, manufacturing and distribution of animal feed.

Hazard analysis and critical control points

Importantly, the Regulation introduces a requirement for FeBOs carrying out any activities beyond primary production to put in place and maintain a written feed safety management system based upon hazard analysis and critical control point (**HACCP**) principles.

HACCP systems are well known as an effective means of maintaining food safety. They involve, broadly speaking, identifying risks – these could be chemical, physical or biological in nature – assessing how those risks can be mitigated or eliminated and the key points at which intervention is needed to do so, having remedial plans in place in case something goes wrong, and keeping records which show that the system is working to deliver safe animal feed.

As an example, a critical control point for raw petfood would be the temperature at which the food becomes prone to microbiological contamination; the mitigation is temperature-controlled processing, storage and distribution.

Registration or Approval

The Regulation provides that FeBOs must register their feed businesses with their local feed authority. This is usually the local authority in whose area the feed business establishment is situated.

For certain activities, namely the manufacturing of feed additives, premixtures and compound feed, the FeBO must, before commencing operations, have their feed business establishment approved by their local feed authority. The feed authority must conduct a site visit prior to the granting of approval. The approval itself can be a full approval (where the FeBO can demonstrate that it complies with all the relevant requirements of feed law), or conditional. A conditional approval may be granted where the feed authority considers that the FeBO meets all the infrastructure and equipment requirements, but that its feed safety management system is not yet fit for purpose.

The Regulation also covers the development of good practice guides, which are to be produced as a joint endeavour by feed businesses and the Food Standards Agency (**FSA**) and/or Food Standards Scotland (**FSS**).

Feed additives

Assimilated Regulation (EC) 1831/2003

Feed additives are governed by Assimilated Regulation (EC) 1831/2003 on additives for use in animal nutrition. The Regulation defines feed additives as substances, micro-organisms or preparations, other than feed material and premixtures, which are intentionally added to feed or water in order to perform, in particular, one or more specific functions. These functions are to:

- Favourably affect the characteristics of feed.
- Favourably affect the characteristics of animal products.
- Favourably affect the colour of ornamental fish and birds.
- Satisfy the nutritional needs of animals.
- Favourably affect the environmental consequences of animal production.

- Favourably affect animal production, performance or welfare, particularly by affecting the gastro-intestinal flora or digestibility of feedingstuffs.

- Have a coccidiostatic or histomonostatic effect (these effects refer to control of parasitic diseases in various farmed animals).

The last function can involve the use of antibiotics, but otherwise antibiotics cannot be authorised as feed additives under the Regulation.

Scientific risk assessment and market authorisation

The Regulations sets out the conditions under which feed additives can lawfully be placed on the market. Put simply, a feed additive must undergo a scientific risk assessment before it can receive authorisation (by a minister) to be used as such, and, in deciding whether to grant an authorisation, and under what conditions, ministers must take into account the opinion of the FSA or FSS. That opinion will consider various matters, including the function the additive is to fulfil, the animal species for which the additive is to be used; post-market monitoring requirements, and whether minimum residue limits for the presence of the additive in foodstuffs derived from the animal should be provided for in the authorisation.

Feed additive authorisations used to be time-limited to a ten-year duration, but following recent changes made by the Food and Feed (Regulated Products) (Amendment, Revocation, Consequential and Transitional Provision) Regulations 2025 (S.I. 2025/361) the authorisation now continues until revoked or modified.

Genetically modified feed

Assimilated Regulation (EC) No. 1829/2003

The use of genetically modified organisms (**GMOs**) in animal feed is dealt with in Assimilated Regulation (EC) No. 1829/2003 on genetically modified food and feed.

Assimilated Regulation (EC) No. 1830/2003, in turn, concerns the traceability and labelling of GMOs and the traceability of food and feed products derived from them.

Genetically modified feed is covered by Chapter III of Regulation 1829/2003. The Regulation is cast broadly so that it covers GMOs for feed use, feed containing or consisting of GMOs; and feed produced from GMOs. Its requirements include that GM feeds must nor have adverse effects on human or animal health or the environment, nor be nutritiously disadvantageous for animals or humans when considered in light of the feed it is intended to replace. No one can place a GM feed on the market unless they have proven by way of evidence supplied to the FSA and/or FSS that the feed meets these requirements, and the feed has been authorised by use by ministers in the light of a scientific risk assessment carried out by the FSA and/or FSS.

The authorisation of a GM feed is currently granted by way of an official publication which sets out the terms of the authorisation and the conditions upon which it is authorised, including the unique identifier of the GM feed, its labelling and the method of detection to be used for its identification. As with the case of feed additives, GM feed authorisations used to be valid for a period of ten years and subject to renewal, but this changed with the coming into force of the Food and Feed (Regulated Products) (Amendment, Revocation, Consequential and Transitional Provision) Regulations 2025 (S.I.

2025/361). By virtue of the amendments made by these Regulations, GM feed authorisations now continue until they are revoked or modified. The details of the GM feed are published on a register maintained by the FSA.

Labelling of GM feed

There are important labelling requirements for GM feed. These are set out in Assimilated Regulation (EC) No. 1830/2003.

In broad terms, FeBOs must label pre-packaged feed (or supply an accompanying statement with any display in which feed is sold loose) with the words 'This product contains genetically modified organisms' or 'This product contains genetically modified [name of organism(s)]'.

In addition, FeBOs must ensure that at each marketing stage before the final sale to a consumer, they provide the receiving FeBO with a written indication of each of the feed materials or additives which is produced from GMOs.

Animal Feed Basic Safety Standards

One of the final pieces of EU legislation relating to animal feed to which the UK gave effect prior to EU Exit was Council Directive 2013/59/Euratom laying down basic safety standards for protection against the dangers arising from exposure to ionising radiation. This Directive consolidated and updated EU Law relating to medical, occupational and public radiation exposures and aimed to provide basic safety standards for the protection of human health in those settings. It drew upon developments at the international level involving recommendations and standards issued by the International Commission on Radiological Protection and the International Atomic

Energy Agency. The Directive's scope included consumer goods, cosmetics as well as food and animal feed. So far as animal feed was concerned, the Directive required member States to prohibit the deliberate addition of radioactive substances in the production of animal feeding stuffs, and to prohibit the import or export of such products.

The use of Directives by the EU allowed Member States some flexibility as to how, as a matter of national law, the requirements of the Directive in question were met. However, over the course of its EU membership, the UK became keen to ensure that it neither under, nor over, implemented the EU's requirements; the former situation creating the risk of the EU launching infraction proceedings against the UK for breach of its duty to properly transpose the requirements of EU law; with the latter risking political agitation that the UK was allowing the overreach of the EU into UK policy areas beyond the EU's legal competence. The UK normally achieved this balancing act by a process of "*copy-out*", whereby it simply lifted the legislative language of the Directive and included it in transcribing domestic legislation. This domestic legislation usually took the form of a statutory instrument made under section 2(2) of the ECA. This was largely the approach taken in relation to the feed aspects of the Directive, with the transcribing measure in England being the Animal Feed (Basic Safety Standards) (England) Regulations 2019 (S.I. 2019/683). Comparable regulations exist in the devolved nations.

Animal Feed (Basic Safety Standards) (England) Regulations

The Animal Feed (Basic Safety Standards) (England) Regulations (**Regulations**) make it a criminal offence in England for any person to intentionally add a radioactive substance in the production of animal feed. The Regulations also make it an offence for any person to import or export any animal feed in respect of which a radioactive substance has been intentionally added in the production of that feed.

The offence is punishable on summary conviction by a fine or, on a second or subsequent conviction, by a fine or imprisonment or both. The Regulations are enforced by the relevant local authority acting in its guise as a feed authority.

Warranty of fitness

While many of the additional enactments governing feed are of EU origin, there is one which is purely domestic and is often forgotten about. Under section 72 of the Agriculture Act 1970 (**AA 1970**), a warranty is implied on behalf of the seller of any material for use as animal feed that the material is suitable to be used as feed. Where the feed is intended for animals of a particular kind, the warranty only extends to the feeding of those kinds of animals. And, where the feed is intended to be mixed with something else before being fed to animals, the warranty does not cover the feed without that mixing having taken place.

It is not possible for the seller of the feed to exclude the warranty by inclusion of contract terms to that effect, nor can a seller exclude the warranty by notice to a buyer.

In any proceedings brought by a buyer of animal feed against a seller relating to an alleged breach of contract, the warranty could be relied upon as a contractual duty owed to the buyer, and breach of which would entitle the buyer to damages in certain circumstances. This is a very useful device and its presence in feed legislation has no clear analogue in food law. Outside of the pet food sector sales of animal feed are more usually business-to-business sales, and in bulk amounts. Thus, for animal feed sales, litigation stemming from alleged breaches of contract is much more likely than in the case of food sales, where individual consumers buy small amounts of food and legal actions for breach of contract are uncommon.

Transmissible Spongiform Encephalopathies

A Transmissible Spongiform Encephalopathy (**TSE**) is a type of disease that affects the brain and nervous system of susceptible animals, including humans. We have already examined, in Chapter Two, its arguably most well-known example, Bovine Spongiform Encephalitis (**BSE**). Other types of TSE include scrapie in sheep and goats and Chronic Wasting Disease in deer. These TSEs cause serious illness and eventual death. The main legal measure dealing with TSEs in animal feed is Assimilated Regulation (EC) No. 999/2001 laying down rules for the prevention, control and eradication of certain TSEs.

Assimilated Regulation (EC) No. 999/2001

Regulation (EC) No. 999/2001 sets out various requirements applying both to the government authorities and to FeBOs. These requirements include:

- An annual monitoring programme, which must be carried out by the appropriate government authority.
- Breeding programmes aimed at lessening the susceptibility of animals to TSEs.
- A prohibition on the feeding of animal proteins to ruminants, and to certain other animal species subject to the provisions set out in Annex IV of the Regulation.

- Controls relating to import and export, including of feed intended for farmed animals which contains protein derived from mammals from countries, or regions of countries, with an undetermined BSE risk.

- Controls relating to 'specified risk materials' (**SRM**), which includes the brain, spinal cord, eyes and tonsils of bovine animals aged over 12 months, and the vertebral column of bovine animals aged over 30 months.

- An obligation on any person who suspects an animal of being infected by a TSE to immediately notify the relevant government authority.

Annex IV of the Regulation deals specifically with the feeding of animals. The Annex sets out some exceptions.

Provision for enforcement of Regulation (EC) No. 999/2001 is made in England by way of the Transmissible Spongiform Encephalopathies (England) Regulations 2018 (S.I. 2018/731). Under those Regulations, a failure by a FeBO to comply with any of the TSE requirements can result in movement restrictions of affected livestock by means of a formal notice and the FeBO is also risk of prosecution for an offence liable on summary conviction to a fine. Comparable regulations exist in the devolved nations.

The scope and nature of the TSE restrictions were examined in the case of *R. (on the application of Banks) v Secretary of State for the Environment, Food and Rural Affairs* [2004] EWHC 416. Here, the claimants were farmers who were suspected of feeding their beef herd with pet food containing mammalian protein. A Department for Environment, Food and Rural Affairs (**Defra**) veterinary official served formal notices under predecessor Regulations to the Transmissible Spongiform Encephalopathies (England) Regulations

2018. These notices prevented the claimants from consigning their herd for food production.

The claimants sought a judicial review of Defra's decision and were successful in persuading the Court that there had been serious shortcomings in procedural fairness on the part of the Secretary of State. These shortcomings included a failure to ask relevant questions of the claimants, a failure to disclose relevant evidence to the claimants, and over stating the nature of the evidence. In the event, by the time of the Court hearing, Defra had already lifted restrictions on the herd and so no relief was needed. In giving judgment in favour of the claimants, the Court commented upon the very serious risks which the TSE Regulations were designed to address, but noted that the absence of any formal right of appeal (at that time) meant that elementary procedural fairness in the course of any investigation, which was lacking in this case, was essential.

Animal by-products

Under food law in the UK, animal by-products can never be classified, or used, as a food. But the same is not true for animal feed. Certain animal products can be used to excellent economic effect as a source of pet food.

The main legislation governing animal by-products is Assimilated Regulation (EC) No. 1069/2009 laying down health rules as regards animal by-products, and the Animal By-Products (Enforcement) (England) Regulations 2013.

Animal by-products (**ABP**) are things which are derived from animals – such as carcases, body parts, skin, bone, blood, hooves, feathers, bristles – but are not intended for the human food-chain.

Assimilated Regulation (EC) No. 1069/2009

Broadly speaking Regulation 1069/2009 classifies ABP into three categories according to risk:

Category 1 is the highest risk; it includes:

- Carcases and parts of animals suspected of being infected with TSE.
- SRM (parts of animals that pose a particular disease risk, e.g. spinal cords).
- Carcases of wild animals suspected of being infected with a disease that humans or animals could catch.
- Parts of animals that are contaminated due to illegal treatments (e.g. unauthorised veterinary medicines).
- Parts of animals that have come into contact with SRM.

Category 2 is also high risk (but moderately less so than Category 1); it includes:

- Animals and parts of animals that die other than by being slaughtered for human consumption, including those killed for disease control purposes (unless these fall into Category 1) and foetuses.
- Unhatched poultry which died in its shell.
- Products containing residues of authorised veterinary drugs and contaminants exceeding the permitted levels.

- Products unfit for human consumption due to the presence of foreign bodies.

- Manure and digestive tract contents.

- Blood from any animal which has not passed ante-mortem inspection.

- Mixtures of Category 2 material with Category 3 material.

Category 3 materials, which are seen as lower risk, and include:

- Carcases or body parts fit for humans to eat but withdrawn for commercial reasons.

- Shells from shellfish with soft tissue.

- Eggs, egg by-products, hatchery by-products and eggshells.

- Aquatic animals, aquatic and terrestrial invertebrates.

- Hides and skins from slaughterhouses.

The use of ABP is strictly controlled. These controls include the measures described below.

ABP must generally be stained with a colourant such that the ABP is (and remains) clearly visually identifiable.

Category 1 and Category 2 ABP can be put to only limited uses including as alternative fuel sources, and for processing into highly refined products such as medical and cosmetic products provided that no unacceptable risks to public and animal health arise.

Category 3 material can, however, be put to wider use. This includes, subject to certain conditions, processing into pet food, which can include both raw and dry pet foods.

Businesses which process ABP, including those which manufacture pet food, must put in place a hygiene management procedure based upon hazard analysis and critical control point (**HACCP**) principles.

It is very important to be aware that, with very limited exceptions, ABP cannot be fed to animals of the species from which the ABP derives.

Enforcement of the provisions of Regulation 1069/2009 is dealt with in England by Animal By-Products (Enforcement) (England) Regulations 2013 (S.I. 2013/2952). These Regulations, broadly speaking, make it an offence to fail to comply with the animal by-product requirements set out in Regulation 1069/2009. The identity of the enforcement authority varies depending upon the type of FeBO involved in the alleged breach – for offences said to have been committed in a slaughterhouse, game handling establishment or cutting plant, the enforcement authority is the FSA; for other premises, the enforcement authority will normally be the local authority, acting in its guise as a feed authority. Comparable regulations exist in the devolved nations.

Imports and exports of animal feed

The law relating to imports and exports of animal feed is complex. This book does not attempt to set out the legal position in full but does offer a road map of the relevant provisions so that time is saved in reaching a view on the specific issues which are likely to arise in practice.

Imports

The most useful starting point when considering imports of animal feed is General Food Law Regulation (EC) No. 178/2002. Under Article 11, feed imported into Great Britain (**GB**) must comply with relevant requirements of food law, or conditions recognised by GB to be at least equivalent to those requirements. This means, put simply, that imported feed must, at the point of import, meet all the domestic regulatory requirements relating to safety, labelling and composition set out elsewhere in this book. This sets a high (but perfectly understandable) threshold for the quality and standards of imported feed.

At a more granular level, the law distinguishes between imports of feed containing products of animal origin (**POAO**) and those which do not.

For POAO, it is important to understand the provisions of Assimilated Regulation (EC) No. 1069/2009 relating animal by-products (mentioned above). The Regulation deals slightly differently with feed for farmed animals and pet food, and also for materials intended for use in the production of dry feeds and those for use in producing raw pet food. However, in all cases, imported feed or feed materials containing POAO must come from countries included on a list maintained by Defra and/or the Animal and Plant Health Agency (**APHA**) and, under Assimilated Implementing Regulation (EU) No. 142/2011, originate from an establishment, plant or operator approved for export to GB (again a list can be found on-line, published by Defra/APHA).

In all cases, the feed containing POAO must be accompanied by a relevant Export Health Certificate (**EHC**) in accordance with Article 31 of Regulation (EU) No. 142/2011 and its arrival in Great Britain (which must be by way of a Border Control Post (**BCP**)) notified in advance to the GB authorities using a dedicated online system known as the "*Import of Products, Animals, Food and Feed System*" (**IPAFFS**). A BCP is any UK port authorised to received consignments of animals, plants and derived products. A list of BCPs can be found online.

The provisions of Regulation 1069/2011 and Regulation 142/2011, so far as they relate to imports of feed containing POAO, are enforced in England mainly by way of the Trade in Animals and Related Products Regulations 2011 (**TARP**) (S.I. 2011/1197). The TARP Regulations, broadly speaking, make it an offence to fail to comply with the import requirements described above, with the enforcement authority generally being the local authority acting in its guise as a port health authority at the relevant BCP. The port health authority has power under regulation 20 of the TARP Regulations to officially detain non-compliant feed products at the border and to order that they be destroyed, re-dispatched outside GB or subject to special treatment. A person who wishes to appeal against the actions of the port health authority has a right of appeal to the magistrate's court under regulation 24 of the TARP Regulations. Comparable regulations exist in the devolved nations.

So far as the import of feed not containing POAO is concerned, the requirements are less exacting. Feed not containing POAO does not need to be sourced from approved overseas producers, nor will pre-notification via IPAFFS or EHCs be required. The only exception to this is where the feed contains what is known as "*high risk food not of animal origin*" (**HRFNAO**).

HRFNAO includes feed which contains certain non-animal derived ingredients (leaf crops/vegetables/nuts) known to be high risk to human health. These ingredients may contain high levels of aflatoxins (a cancer-implicated poison created by certain types of mould), excessive pesticide residues, or microbiological contamination.

Current restrictions include groundnut flours and feed cake. Some HRFNAO cannot be imported to GB at all, while others are subject to special conditions of entry such as, for example, providing results of sampling and analysis performed on the HRFNAO by the competent authorities of the country of origin. The arrival of HRFNAO into GB must be pre-notified to the competent authorities by means of IPAFFS and the HRFNAO must be imported through a BCP.

The main legislation governing import of HRFNAO is Assimilated Regulation (EU) 2019/1793. The Regulation's Annexes set out the affected ingredients in tabular form. The Regulation is enforced in England by way of the Official Feed and Food Controls (England) Regulations 2009 (S.I. 2009/3255). These Regulations, among other things, provide at regulation 32 for port health authorities to serve notices on an importer of feed which does not comply with feed law, requiring it to destroy the feed, re-dispatch the feed outside GB, or subject the feed to special treatment. The importer has a right of appeal to the magistrate's court under regulation 33. Comparable regulations exist in the devolved nations.

Exports

Exports of feed, so far as they involve export to an EU Member State, largely reflect the import requirements, but in reverse.

The starting point for exports of feed from GB is therefore Assimilated Regulation (EC) No. 178/2002 (General Food Law). Article 12 requires that feed exported from GB for placing on the market of a third country must comply with relevant requirements of food law. This is subject to the exception that unsafe feed can be exported to a third country if the competent authorities in that country have been properly informed of the circumstances and have expressly agreed to receive the feed.

So far as feed that contains POAO is concerned, the UK is currently listed by the EU as a third country from which imports of POAO can be received. But it is necessary also for the establishment, plant or producer of the feed to be listed an approved site for the purposes of export of the feed to the EU. The feed must comply with the requirements of the EU law versions of Regulation (EC) No. 1069/2009 and of Implementing Regulation (EU) No. 142/2011 and to be imported through a BCP located in an EU Member State. The exporting FeBO will need to have an EHC completed before export, and the arrival of the consignment of exported feed must be pre-notified to the EU using the EU's Trade Control and Expert System (**Traces**).

Conclusion

Beyond the basic obligations contained in the General Food Law Regulation (EC) No. 178/2002, there are a range of specific and detailed legal requirements affecting feed. Many of these additional obligations set clear parameters for what feed can be made of, how it can be packaged, and what information or labelling must accompany it. In addition, there is now detailed provision governing the hygienic production and handling of feed, an area which, until 2005, had received little attention from UK lawmakers.

It is these specific requirements which, perhaps, elevate feed law from merely an aspect of the wider topic of food law, and give it shape as a distinct area of specialism and expertise.

CHAPTER FIVE

OFFICIAL CONTROLS AND ENFORCEMENT

Introduction

Having now looked at the main substance of animal feed law, we can concern ourselves with the important topic of how that law is enforced.

The development of the internal market of the EU – and the increasingly prescriptive nature of EU law which was required to harmonise the laws of member States trading within it – has profoundly shaped the nature of feed law enforcement. Increasingly, prescription took the form of a gradual switch by the EU from Directives, (which set out the '*end*' but not the '*means*' of internal market measures), to Regulations (which were directly applicable in Member States and left them no discretion as to end or means).

However, EU Regulations stopped short of including detailed measures relating to their enforcement, meaning that Member States had to enact domestic enforcement measures which supplemented the relevant EU Regulation. This had the unwelcome effect of creating a legislative scheme for feed which compromised more than one type of enactment; and, indeed, more than one system of law.

The decoupling of substantive measures from their enforcing measures makes for a complex picture. Over time, we might hope to see some streamlining and merger of feed law back into seamless national measures but, for the time being at least, practitioners need to be able to plot a course through the thicket.

Official controls

So, what is an "*official control*"? Broadly speaking an official control is any activity performed by a government authority to confirm that a Feed Business Operator (**FeBO**) is meeting all the legal requirements relating to feed. By and large, these controls are performed by the local authority in whose geographical area the FeBO's establishment is located.

These activities may include unannounced inspections of feed manufacturing sites to check that machinery, equipment and processes meet the necessary requirements, laboratory sampling and analysis of feed to identify any adulteration, contaminants or unauthorised presence of genetically modified (**GM**) ingredients, review of labelling to ensure that accurate information is being provided, and review of traceability requirements to ensure that feed can be traced back to source or forward to customers (other than the final consumer).

The detailed basis for official controls, and how they are to be performed, is set out in Assimilated Regulation (EU) 2017/625 (**Official Controls Regulation**). If an official control reveals that a FeBO has failed to comply with any aspect of feed law, the local authority has various powers of enforcement. These powers are considered, below.

Enforcement

The main provisions relating to enforcement of animal feed law are contained in secondary legislation.

When it comes to enforcement, the now historic distinction between directly applicable EU regulations (creating the substance of feed law) and domestic secondary legislation (by which that substance is enforced) can create a trap for the unwary. This is particularly so when considering the detail of the Official Controls Regulation.

The Official Controls Regulation is a substantial enactment and deals comprehensively with a range of issues relating to enforcement of food, animal feed and plant health law. This includes official controls relating to production, hygiene, imports, the designation of enforcement authorities, the delegation of official control tasks, reference laboratories, multi-annual national control plans and a range of other matters.

While the Official Controls Regulation almost certainly deals with the type of enforcement activity which most feed practitioners come across in practice, the important question is not *whether* it deals with it, but *how* it deals with it. Many of the Official Control Regulation's provisions were aimed at securing the compliance of the Member State with its own obligations under EU food and feed law, rather than at the activities of a FeBO.

The Animal Feed (Composition, Marketing and Use) (England) Regulations 2015

So far as the key obligations contained in Regulation 178/2002 General Food Law are concerned, the main enforcing provision in England is the Animal Feed (Composition, Marketing and Use) (England) Regulations 2015. These Regulations make it an offence, among other things, to place unsafe feed on the market, to fail to withdraw and recall unsafe feed and/or to fail to inform competent authorities of the withdrawal and recall. If the offence is proven, penalties include a term of imprisonment not exceeding 3 months or an unlimited fine, or both. Comparable regulations exist in the devolved nations.

As regards to the requirements relating to the composition, marketing and use of feed set out in Regulation 767/2009, and the requirements of Regulation 1829/2003 relating to genetically modified feed, the main enforcing provision in England is also the Animal Feed (Composition, Marketing and Use) (England) Regulations 2015. If offences are proven in respect of any of these areas, penalties similarly include a term of imprisonment not exceeding 3 months or an unlimited fine, or both.

The Animal Feed (Hygiene, Sampling etc. and Enforcement) (England) Regulations 2015

So far as feed hygiene provisions are concerned, provision for enforcement in England is made by way of the Animal Feed (Hygiene, Sampling etc. and Enforcement) (England) Regulations 2015. These Regulations provide that a failure to comply with the feed hygiene requirements is punishable as an offence on (a) summary conviction to a term of imprisonment not exceeding 3 months or to an unlimited fine, or both; (b) on conviction on indictment to a term of imprisonment not exceeding 2 years or an unlimited fine, or both. Comparable regulations exist in the devolved nations.

Interestingly, the Animal Feed (Hygiene, Sampling etc. and Enforcement) (England) Regulations 2015 contain a potential defence to any criminal charge which may be brought under them in the form of what is known as a *"due diligence"* defence.

Put simply, to rely on the due diligence defence, it is vital that the FeBO has a robust feed safety management system in place which includes appropriate checks and balances. The system – which must apply to the whole range of activities carried out by the FeBO – must be written down; understood by staff who have been fully trained on it; be capable of proactively preventing problems, and of resolving them if they do arise. In situations where important ingredients are sourced from another supplier, it will require periodic and effective sampling to be carried out on the safety of that supplier's products, and perhaps some assessment of the quality standards and systems of those who are further upstream, such as primary producers or importers.

A good feed safety management system is vital for any FeBO faced with an accusation that it has committed a criminal offence, and is also key to successfully defending any civil action which an injured buyer or consumer may bring against the feed business.

Feed hygiene provisions also involve a range of enforcement measures beyond criminal prosecution. These include certain statutory notices such as Feed Business Improvement Notices, Feed Business Emergency Prohibition Notices, and Detention Notices.

These notices, respectively, allow an enforcement authority to specify how a FeBO is failing to comply with feed law and specify steps the FeBO must take to put that right, to take emergency action to stop a feed business operating where the enforcement authority considers that the FeBO's activities create an imminent risk of injury to health (and health means the health of an animal or, through the consumption of the products of such animal, human health).

An enforcement authority can also seize and detain products where the enforcement authority considers that certain feed fails to comply with feed law. The power to seize and detain is subject to the supervisory jurisdiction of a magistrates' court. A magistrates' court has the role of either conforming or discharging the Detention Notice. If the court fails to confirm the notice, the FeBO has a right to compensation from the enforcement authority for any loss in value of the feed caused by its detention.

Other enforcement measures

These are not the only measures which deal with the enforcement of feed law. Some of the wider legislation affecting animal feed, such as the Transmissible Spongiform Encephalopathy (**TSE**) legislation and Animal by-products (**ABP**) legislation are subject to separate enforcement measures such as the Transmissible Spongiform Encephalopathies (England) Regulations 2018 and the Animal By-Products (Enforcement) (England) Regulations 2013. We are not able to cover the detail of these enforcement measures in a book of this size and nature, but practitioners should familiarise themselves with the measures and be aware that they will govern important aspects of the matters which their clients will encounter if questions arise about regulatory compliance.

Feed authorities

The main enforcing regulations, mentioned above, set out who is empowered to act as the enforcement authority. Normally, this is the local authority in whose geographical area the FeBO's establishment is located, but in certain circumstances elements of feed law can be enforced by persons appointed by the Secretary of State. The regulations adopt the definition of "feed authority" for enforcement purposes, and this definition generally refers to those local authorities identified in section 67(1) of the Agriculture Act 1970 (**AA 1970**) as having the duty to enforce Part IV of that Act within their areas or districts.

When reading the enforcement regulations, it is important to distinguish between "competent authorities" and "enforcement authorities". This because the regulations tend to deal with the role of each type of authority differently, depending upon the nature of the regulatory function (under the relevant assimilated law) which the particular authority is to perform. Under the enforcement regulations, "competent authorities" tend to be empowered to perform some function which does not involve enforcement, typically this could some form of compliance monitoring or similar activity.

In practice, where a FeBO is responding to a compliance query from a governmental body, it is always sensible to check whether the government body in question is actually empowered under legislation as the enforcement authority for the measure being investigated. Also, the individual government official who raises those queries must be properly authorised under the specific legislation in question before they have a legal basis for their activities.

The hierarchy of enforcement

While, as we have explored above, the enforcement measures relating to feed law are many and varied – covering both criminal sanctions and civil notices – the starting point in relation to any regulatory breach should be education rather than enforcement. Only in the event of serious and continued breaches should formal enforcement measures be contemplated. And these enforcement measures should, in general, be used sparingly and should progress from the least to the most punitive in accordance with the seriousness of the breach in question. This is known as the "*hierarchy of enforcement*".

The hierarchy is more than just a working practice. It is given a degree of formal status by virtue of its inclusion in the statutory Feed Law Code of Practice for England (**Code**). The Code describes the hierarchy in the following terms:

"Competent Authorities must ensure:

- *their authorised officers take account of the full range of enforcement options available to them;*

- *their officers operate a graduated and educative approach (the hierarchy of enforcement) starting with advice (which Competent Authorities may charge for) and informal action moving to more formal action, where the informal action does not achieve the desired effect, except where circumstances indicate a significant or imminent risk to public and / or animal health, food or feed safety; and*

- *the approach taken results in the timely remedy of non-compliance with feed law.".*

While the Code – and the hierarchy of enforcement which it advocates – is not legally binding on feed authorities, it must be taken into account by feed authorities in performing their functions. If a feed authority fails to do so, the Food Standards Agency (**FSA**) is empowered, having consulted the Secretary of State, to give a feed authority a direction requiring them to take specified steps to comply with the Code.

Earned recognition

In recent years, the FSA has promoted schemes of third-party assurance for certain food and feed sectors. These schemes, known as "*earned recognition*" aim to reduce official inspection frequences and to target enforcement authority resources on food and feed businesses with poorer records of compliance. A scheme for feed was adopted by the FSA in 2014.

Under the scheme, the FSA, along with Food Standards Scotland (**FSS**) and the Veterinary Medicines Directorate of the Department for Environment, Food and Rural Affairs (**Defra**), entered into a memorandum of understanding with the Agricultural Industries Confederation (**AIC**). The AIC is an independent, not-for-profit organisation that works on behalf of members in the agricultural supply sector. The AIC represents a variety of sectors within the feed industry and manages several assurance schemes, which include the Feed Materials Assurance Scheme (**FEMAS**); the Trade Assurance Scheme for Combinable Crops (**TASCC**); and the Universal Feed Assurance Scheme (**UFAS**).

The FSA has indicated that feed authorities are to ensure that, where a FeBO loses earned recognition under one of the assurance schemes, they notify the FSA as soon as possible. The FSA has stated that the purpose of this "exception" reporting is so that it can perform a "verifying" role in relation to the assurance schemes.

Conclusion

Non-compliance with feed law has serious consequences for FeBOs. Non-compliance can be a criminal offence and carry with it the possibility of fines and even imprisonment. The damage caused to a FeBO's reputation by a criminal prosecution, whether or not a conviction follows, can be serious and in some cases, irreparable.

It therefore pays for FeBOs to maintain a good relationship with their local feed authorities and also to challenge any disproportionate or precipitous action which an authorised officer may take which fails to properly reflect the hierarchy of enforcement.

In the event that criminal proceedings are, ultimately, brought against the FeBO, depending on the offence charged, the FeBO may be able to rely upon a due diligence defence to avoid a damaging and potentially costly conviction.

CHAPTER SIX

SAMPLING AND ANALYSIS

Introduction

The complexity of certain aspects of feed safety, particularly those relating to chemical or biological contamination, demand some precision in relation to feed sampling and analysis.

Scientific analysis of food samples can trace its history to the middle part of the 19th century. The Adulteration of Food and Drugs Act 1860 provided for the appointment of analysts, who were to issue certificates indicating whether food was adulterated and/or injurious to health. The role of food analysts developed over time to become the Public Analyst Scientific Service (**PASS**) with which we are familiar, today.

However, comparable steps in relation to the analysis of feed are somewhat more recent. While chemists were certainly assisting with analysis of feed and fertilizers from at least the early years of the 20th century, the office of Agricultural Analyst does not appear to have been created until the Agriculture Act 1970 (**AA 1970**).

Today, PASS carry out both food and feed analysis for the purpose of assisting enforcement authorities and its scientists are appointed as Agricultural Analysts under the AA 1970. A brief examination of the some of the provisions follows, below.

Agricultural Analysts

The AA 1970, Part IV provides for the appointment of Agricultural Analysts and Deputy Agricultural Analysts by enforcement authorities. These analysts must hold qualifications which are set out in legislation. At present the qualifications required are, broadly speaking, a Mastership in Chemical Analysis awarded by the Royal Society of Chemistry, or to be a Chartered Chemist and, in either case, also be a Fellow or a Member of the Royal Society of Chemistry.

Certificates of analysis

As the Animal Feed (Composition, Marketing and Use) (England) Regulations 2015 are partly made under powers conferred by the AA 1970, Agricultural Analysts and Deputy Agricultural Analysts appointed under that Act are able to provide scientific and expert opinion in relation to questions arising about compliance of feed with the various requirements of feed law. Indeed, the certificate of analysis by an Agricultural Analyst or the Government Chemist shall, in any legal proceedings, be received as evidence of the facts stated in it, providing the party against whom it is to be relied upon has had adequate notice of it and does not seek to call the chemist as a witness.

The powers contained in the AA 1970 do not extend to feed hygiene and so it was necessary for ministers to make separate provision to appoint Agricultural Analysts for the purpose of expert input on questions of biological risk and related matters. Part 3 of the Animal Feed (Hygiene, Sampling etc. and Enforcement) (England) Regulations 2015 does this neatly and efficiently by deeming the analysts appointed under the AA 1970 to be similarly appointed for the purpose of Regulation 183/2005 and related measures.

As for the taking and handling of samples, section 75 of the AA 1970 provides a purchaser of feed with the right to have a sample of the feed analysed by the Agricultural Analyst appointed for that area. And, under section 76, An authorised officer of the local feed authority has power to enter premises in which feed is held for sale and to take a sample of it for similar analysis.

The process by which samples are taken is carefully set out in the legislation. Broadly speaking, under sections 75 to 79 of the AA 1970, the process requires the authorised officer to divide the sample into three (or four if the manufacturer is not the seller), roughly equal, parts and then seal up and label each part. The authorised officer then must send one part to the Agricultural Analyst, give another part to the seller, another to the manufacturer (where applicable) and retain the final part for a defined period. The purchaser or the seller of the feed can require the feed authority to send the retained part to the Government Chemist for analysis. The retained part therefore operates as a reference sample in case of challenge or dispute about the accuracy of the initial analysis, and the Government Chemist then issues a certificate which is taken as evidence as to the facts stated in it unless the party against whom it is to be relied upon seeks, within a prescribed timescale, to call the Government Chemist (or the Government's Chemist's representative) as a witness.

In broad terms, the process of sampling and analysis described above extends to include matters relating to feed hygiene, although the legislative basis for it is different. In this case, the relevant provisions are found in regulations 15 to 20 of the Animal Feed (Hygiene, Sampling etc. and Enforcement) (England) Regulations 2015. The 2015 Regulations have the advantage of making some provision for analysis carried out otherwise than for the purpose of official controls, by requiring that analysis be performed in accordance with methods set out in Assimilated Regulation (EC) No. 152/2009 laying down the methods of sampling and analysis for the official control of feed.

Conclusion

The role of Agricultural Analysts is extremely important. Scientific and technological developments have made sophisticated inroads into the analysis of feed, with new methods such as whole genome sequencing providing once inconceivable levels of accuracy in relation to the attributes of particular feeds. While this accuracy is welcome – particularly in relation to the prosecution of criminal offences where proof beyond reasonable doubt creates a high evidential threshold – the performance of the analysis and the interpretation of results demands scientific expertise.

It seems correct, therefore, that some benchmarks are set within the regulatory system for levels of qualification to be held by those holding themselves out as Agricultural Analysts, and that the process by which samples are taken for inspection by the Analyst is careful and transparent. Without the latter, the former may fail to secure the policy outcomes which the legislation aims to deliver.

The status of certificates of analysis is also an important feature of feed law enforcement. These certificates can be relied upon as determinative of the facts stated in them in certain circumstances. This eases the burden on the court system and avoids the needs for trials of fact on complex evidence where a court would, in any event, be likely to seek the opinion of an expert.

CHAPTER SEVEN

THE FUTURE REGULATION OF FEED

Introduction

Products of animal origin are an important part of people's diet in the UK. They are a valuable source of nutrients essential to good health. While concerns about the climate impact of animal-derived foods will, no doubt, continue to drive discussion and debate about how to provide for the world's protein needs, the demand for these foods seems more likely to increase as developing nations become wealthier.

At a more regional level, the UK Food Security Report 2024 reveals long term increases in the production of beef, pork and poultry in the UK, with lamb and mutton production remaining largely stable over time. Dairy and egg production has decreased somewhat, with the UK currently being a net importer of eggs and cheese.

An important precursor to all these products of animal origin is, of course, animal feed. The UK does not grow sufficient amounts of protein crops such as peas and beans to meet the demand for feed production, and so the UK imports material amounts of grain and soymeal for these purposes.

The impact of biotechnology

The future is likely to see the growth in development of new protein sources for the purposes of feed production. These may include things such as insect protein and genetically modified or gene edited feeds, whose characteristics are improved so as to reduce the environmental impact of the farmed animals to which they are fed.

Liberalisation of feed controls

There have also been recent considerations about whether to liberalise the longstanding restrictions over the inclusion of animal-derived proteins in feed. This is sensitive topic. As mentioned in Chapter One, the development of Bovine Spongiform Encephalitis (**BSE**) in the UK herd was almost certainly brought about by the since banned practice of including animal proteins in feed fed to animals of the same species from which that protein was derived.

Nevertheless, much time has passed since the 1980s to 1990s during which the BSE crisis was at its peak, and scientific knowledge about Transmissible Spongiform Encephalopathies (**TSEs**), of which BSE is a type, is said to have improved in that time. The Department for Environment, Food and Rural Affairs (**Defra**) have recently claimed that it is now known that poultry and pigs are not naturally prone to TSEs and that feed testing methods have improved to the point at which proteins from different species can be detected and steps could be taken to ensure that protein of a species is not fed to animal of that same species.

Novel proteins

Liberalisation of animal feed controls could see, for example, greater circularisation of resources. A good example of what may be possible here is found in a recent trial which involves the feeding of insects (black soldier fly) with porcine slurry, following which the flies can be harvested to produce edible protein. At present, that protein could not be used for animal feed, given the link back to pig slurry, but that could change in the near future.

While reform of feed controls is now a matter of UK law (at least in England, Scotland and Wales) and any liberalisation a matter for our domestic legislatures, the UK is keeping a close eye on what is happening in the EU. The EU has already begun to make some changes, including an amendment in its TSE legislation to allow the use of a wider range of animal proteins in non-ruminant animal feed.

Climate change

The reality of a currently warming world is that some areas used for the growing and cultivation of feed crops are also becoming wetter. There is some discussion within the scientific community about whether those warmer and wetter conditions are leading to higher levels of crop contamination in the form of mycotoxins.

A mycotoxin is a poison which is produced by certain types of fungus. These fungi commonly grow on foods such as cereals, dried fruit and spices. The growth of these fungi can occur at any stage of the production cycle, pre or post-harvest, during storage or transport. Moist, warm conditions promote their growth. The poison they produce is potent and can cause severe illness in people and animals and can be passed on through contaminated feed. Milk is a particular problem. Most of the common mycotoxins are chemically stable and can therefore remain in a food notwithstanding any processing which it undergoes.

Climate change is also likely to affect the location and productiveness of cultivatable land. This, too, will no doubt have an impact on the balance of land given over to crops intended for feed production, though warming of some areas of northern and southern hemispheres may open up land to farming which had previously been unsuitable for cultivation.

There is also considerable concern about the carbon footprint of many products of animal origin, the footprint of these products being much higher than plant-based alternatives. It is possible that technology will have a role to play in reducing that footprint. We have already seen the successful use of a feed additive for cattle in reducing the amount of methane which the cattle produce, and trials have shown that the additive is safe for use in food-producing animals.

Conclusion

The likely growth in demand for animal feed, and the pressure on resources available for its production, will no doubt drive innovation. This may include biotechnology developments, such as gene editing or more general improvements in the efficiency of agricultural production.

The impact of climate change – and the comparatively high carbon footprint of products of animal origin – will affect animal husbandry, of which feed will play an important part. We have already seen the use of additives in cattle feed being used to reduce that footprint.

Ultimately, the world must continue to produce enough food to meet the needs of its growing population. With products of animal origin continuing to be an important part of the world's diet, the production of animal feed, and its proper regulation, will remain of strategic importance to all of the world's economies.

MORE BOOKS BY LAW BRIEF PUBLISHING

A selection of our other titles available now:-

'A Practical Guide to Probation Breaches and Other Applications' by Mark Thomas
'A Practical Guide to Remarriage and Divorce' by Cordelia Williams & Claire Howard
'A Practical Guide to Privacy, Transparency, Reporting Restrictions and Closed Proceedings in the Court of Protection' by Laura Mannering
'Beaumont on Barristers – A Guide to Defending Disciplinary Proceedings (Second Edition)' by Marc Beaumont
'A Practical Guide to Payments for Environmental Services' by Ben Sharples
'A Practical Guide to the Law of Pregnancy and Maternity at Work' by Rebecca Thomas
'A Practical Guide to Redundancy – Second Edition' by Philip Hyland & Collette Moore
'A Practical Guide to International Issues for Scottish Family Lawyers' by Susie Mountain, Donna McKay, Ken MacDonald
'A Practical Guide to the Law on Deprivation of Liberty' by Ben Troke
'A Practical Guide to Rights over Airspace and Subsoil – Second Edition' by Daniel Gatty
'A Practical Guide to the Law in Relation to Inquests' by Ramya Nagesh
'A Practical Guide to the Construction and Rectification of Wills and Trust Instruments (Second Edition)' by Edward Hewitt
'A Practical Guide to Data Protection in Social Housing' by Clare Paterson
'A Practical Guide to Spousal Maintenance – Second Edition' by Liz Cowell
'A Practical Guide to International Parental Child Abduction Law (England and Wales)' by Dr Onyója Momoh
'A Practical Guide to Deprivation of British Citizenship' by Sean Ell
'A Practical Guide to Commercial Property Service Charges' by Rachel Garton
'A Practical Guide to Clinical Negligence – Third Edition' by Geoffrey Simpson-Scott (Geoff)
'A Practical Guide to the Rights of Grandparents in Children Proceedings – Second Edition' by Stuart Barlow

'The Electronic Communications Code: A Practical Guide – Second Edition' by Kerry Bretherton KC, James Castle, Mark Loveday
'A Practical Guide to the Independent School Standards – September 2023 Edition' by Sarah McKimm
'A Practical Guide to Estate Administration and Crypto Assets' by Richard Marshall
'A Practical Guide to Parental Alienation in Private and Public Law Children Cases' by Sam King QC & Frankie Shama
'Contested Heritage – Removing Art from Land and Historic Buildings' by Richard Harwood QC, Catherine Dobson, David Sawtell
'The Limits of Separate Legal Personality: When Those Running a Company Can Be Held Personally Liable for Losses Caused to Third Parties Outside of the Company' by Dr Mike Wilkinson
'A Practical Guide to Transgender Law' by Robin Moira White & Nicola Newbegin
'A Practical Guide to 'Stranded Spouses' in Family Law' by Mani Singh Basi
'A Practical Guide to Residential Freehold Conveyancing' by Lorraine Richardson
'A Practical Guide to Pensions on Divorce for Lawyers' by Bryan Scant
'A Practical Guide to Challenging Sham Marriage Allegations in Immigration Law' by Priya Solanki
'A Practical Guide to Digital Communications Evidence in Criminal Law' by Sam Willis
'A Practical Guide to Legal Rights in Scotland' by Sarah-Jane Macdonald
'A Practical Guide to New Build Conveyancing' by Paul Sams & Rebecca East
'A Practical Guide to Inherited Wealth on Divorce' by Hayley Trim
'A Practical Guide to Practice Direction 12J and Domestic Abuse in Private Law Children Proceedings' by Rebecca Cross & Malvika Jaganmohan
'A Practical Guide to Confiscation and Restraint' by Narita Bahra QC, John Carl Townsend, David Winch
'A Practical Guide to the Law of Forests in Scotland' by Philip Buchan
'A Practical Guide to Health and Medical Cases in Immigration Law' by Rebecca Chapman & Miranda Butler
'A Practical Guide to Bad Character Evidence for Criminal Practitioners by Aparna Rao
'A Practical Guide to Extradition Law post-Brexit' by Myles Grandison et al
'A Practical Guide to Hoarding and Mental Health for Housing Lawyers' by Rachel Coyle

'Stephens on Contractual Indemnities' by Richard Stephens
'A Practical Guide to the EU Succession Regulation' by Richard Frimston
'A Practical Guide to Solicitor and Client Costs – Second Edition' by Robin Dunne
'Constructive Dismissal – Practice Pointers and Principles' by Benjimin Burgher
'A Practical Guide to Religion and Belief Discrimination Claims in the Workplace' by Kashif Ali
'A Practical Guide to the Law of Medical Treatment Decisions' by Ben Troke
'Fundamental Dishonesty and QOCS in Personal Injury Proceedings: Law and Practice' by Jake Rowley
'A Practical Guide to the Law in Relation to School Exclusions' by Charlotte Hadfield & Alice de Coverley
'A Practical Guide to Divorce for the Silver Separators' by Karin Walker
'The Right to be Forgotten – The Law and Practical Issues' by Melissa Stock
'A Practical Guide to Planning Law and Rights of Way in National Parks, the Broads and AONBs' by James Maurici QC, James Neill et al
'A Practical Guide to Election Law' by Tom Tabori
'A Practical Guide to the Law in Relation to Surrogacy' by Andrew Powell
'A Practical Guide to Claims Arising from Fatal Accidents – Second Edition' by James Patience
'A Practical Guide to Asbestos Claims' by Jonathan Owen & Gareth McAloon
'A Practical Guide to Stamp Duty Land Tax in England and Northern Ireland' by Suzanne O'Hara
'A Practical Guide to the Law of Farming Partnerships' by Philip Whitcomb
'A Practical Guide to the Law of Unlawful Eviction and Harassment – Second Edition' by Stephanie Lovegrove
'A Practical Guide to Costs in Personal Injury Claims – Second Edition' by Matthew Hoe
'A Practical Guide to the General Data Protection Regulation (GDPR) – Second Edition' by Keith Markham
'A Practical Guide to Working with Litigants in Person and McKenzie Friends in Family Cases' by Stuart Barlow
'Protecting Unregistered Brands: A Practical Guide to the Law of Passing Off' by Lorna Brazell
'A Practical Guide to Secondary Liability and Joint Enterprise Post-Jogee' by Joanne Cecil & James Mehigan

'A Practical Guide to the Pre-Action RTA Claims Protocol for Personal Injury Lawyers' by Antonia Ford
'A Practical Guide to Neighbour Disputes and the Law' by Alexander Walsh
'A Practical Guide to Coercive Control for Legal Practitioners and Victims' by Rachel Horman
'A Practical Guide to the Law of Driverless Cars – Second Edition'
by Alex Glassbrook, Emma Northey & Scarlett Milligan
'A Practical Guide to TOLATA Claims' by Greg Williams
'A Practical Guide to Elderly Law – Second Edition' by Justin Patten
'A Practical Guide to Responding to Housing Disrepair and Unfitness Claims' by Iain Wightwick
'A Practical Guide to the Law of Bullying and Harassment in the Workplace' by Philip Hyland
'How to Be a Freelance Solicitor: A Practical Guide to the SRA-Regulated Freelance Solicitor Model' by Paul Bennett
'A Practical Guide to Prison Injury Claims' by Malcolm Johnson
'A Practical Guide to Advising Clients at the Police Station' by Colin Stephen McKeown-Beaumont
'A Practical Guide to Antisocial Behaviour Injunctions – Second Edition' by Iain Wightwick
'Practical Mediation: A Guide for Mediators, Advocates, Advisers, Lawyers, and Students in Civil, Commercial, Business, Property, Workplace, and Employment Cases' by Jonathan Dingle with John Sephton
'The Mini-Pupillage Workbook' by David Boyle
'A Practical Guide to Crofting Law' by Brian Inkster
'A Practical Guide to the Law of Domain Names and Cybersquatting' by Andrew Clemson
'A Practical Guide to the Law of Gender Pay Gap Reporting' by Harini Iyengar
'NHS Whistleblowing and the Law' by Joseph England
'Employment Law and the Gig Economy' by Nigel Mackay & Annie Powell
'A Practical Guide to Noise Induced Hearing Loss (NIHL) Claims' by Andrew Mckie, Ian Skeate, Gareth McAloon
'An Introduction to Beauty Negligence Claims – A Practical Guide for the Personal Injury Practitioner' by Greg Almond
'Intercompany Agreements for Transfer Pricing Compliance' by Paul Sutton
'Zen and the Art of Mediation' by Martin Plowman
'A Practical Guide to Adoption for Family Lawyers' by Graham Pegg

www.ingramcontent.com/pod-product-compliance
Ingram Content Group UK Ltd.
Pitfield, Milton Keynes, MK11 3LW, UK
UKHW020151290926
15471UKWH00004B/808

9 781916 698925